HORRID HENRY'S MIGHTY JOKE BOOK

Francesca Simon spent her childhood on the beach in California, and then went to Yale and Oxford Universities to study medieval history and literature. She now lives in London with her English husband and their son. When she is not writing books she is doing theatre and restaurant reviews or chasing after her Tibetan Spaniel, Shanti.

Tony Ross is one of Britain's best-known illustrators, with many picture books to his name as well as line drawings for many fiction titles. He lives in Cheshire.

Also by Francesca Simon

Complete list of *Horrid Henry*
titles at the end of the book

Don't Cook Cinderella
Helping Hercules

and for younger readers
Don't Be Horrid, Henry
Spider School

HORRID HENRY'S MIGHTY JOKE BOOK

Francesca Simon

Illustrated by Tony Ross

Orion
Children's Books

First published in Great Britain in 2008
by Orion Children's Books
a division of the Orion Publishing Group Ltd
Orion House
5 Upper Saint Martin's Lane
London WC2H 9EA
An Hachette Livre UK Company

www.orionbooks.co.uk
www.horridhenry.co.uk

For my very own Jolly Josh

CONTENTS

HORRID HENRY'S MIGHTY JOKE BOOK

Isn't that typical? You have the brilliant, wonderful, spectacular idea of writing a joke book, and then suddenly EVERYONE wants to do it. What they don't know is that I saved my best horrid jokes. And my best skeleton jokes. And my best school jokes. This joke book is ALL mine! I can do whatever I want! Which means I get to keep *all* the money!!! No more sharing!

Because I have had a brilliant, spectacular idea. I'll charge everybody hundreds of pounds to have their name in my book.

Then I'll charge them hundreds of pounds to *buy* the book. I'm going to buy 30 TVs and 5 computers and the Frosty Freeze ice cream factory.

And since I've chosen the very best jokes for a few friends (and evil enemies) they'll be sure to buy loads of copies!

JOSH'S JOLLY JOKES

If you don't laugh out loud at Josh's jolly jokes I'll—I'll—I'll give Peter £3. Actually make that £1. No, 25p. Hmm, wait, I have a better idea. I'll make Peter give me 50p every time you laugh. So get laughing.

Why was the computer cold?
It forgot to close its windows.

What did the hungry computer say?
I could go for a byte.

Who is Snow White's brother?
Egg white. Get the yolk?

Where is Captain Hook's treasure chest?
Under his treasure shirt.

What did one shoelace say to the other shoelace?
That's knot mine.

Why did Mrs Grape leave Mr Grape?
She was tired of raisin kids.

Why couldn't the sailors play cards?
Because the captain was on the deck.

What do jokes and pencils have in common?
They're no good without a point.

What will they do when the Forth Bridge collapses?
Build a fifth bridge.

What do you say to a chicken before a performance?
Break an egg.

Why shouldn't you play cards in the jungle?
There are too many cheetahs.

What do you call a naughty monkey?
A badboon.

Why did the fly go to Paris?
He wanted to become a French fly.

Why do chickens watch television?
For hen–tertainment.

What do you use to fix a broken tooth?
Toothpaste.

Do you know me?
Yes.
Knock knock.
Who's there?
I thought you knew me.

How does an Eskimo build his house?
Igloos it together.

What monster dances the best?
The bogey man.

What happened to the magic tractor?
It went down the lane and turned into a field.

What can make grass grow bigger?
Magnifiying Grass.

Why does a cow moo?
Because its horns don't work.

Knock knock.
Who's there?
Too whit.
Too whit who?
Is there an owl in the house?

*What was Humpty
Dumpty wearing when
he fell?*
A shellsuit.

Knock knock.
Who's there?
Turner.
Turner who?
Turner round there's a monster.

Why do birds fly south?
Because it's too far to walk.

Knock knock.
Who's there?
Chile.
Chile who?
Chile being an abominable snowman.

KATE'S KUNG-FU JOKES

I'll keep well away from Kate and her kung-fu chops when she reads these magnificent martial arts jokes. Haiiiiiii-ya!

What happened when the karate champion joined the army and saluted?
He nearly killed himself.

What lives in a pod and is a kung-fu expert?
Bruce pea.

Why are the Olympic qualifiers in kung-fu so hot?
Because there is hardly a fan in the place.

What do you get when you cross a karate expert with a pig?
Pork chops.

What does a martial arts fan eat?
Kung food.

Why was the sword swallower sent to prison?
He coughed and killed two people.

VIOLET'S VAIN JOKES

Henry, do I get to see my jokes before you put them in?

Violet, I'm insulted. You'll love the jokes, promise. Now pay up.

Why did Violet join the Navy?
So the world could see her.

Why doesn't a bald man have any keys?
Because he has no locks.

What do you call a very popular perfume?
A best–smeller.

VIOLET: Is that perfume I smell?
MARGARET: It is, and yes, you do.

VIOLET: I'm all red and blistered from sitting in the sun.
HENRY: Well, I guess you basked for it.

VIOLET: Did you see me at the beauty contest?
HENRY: On and off.
VIOLET: How did you like me?
HENRY: Off.

14

JIM'S JAZZY JOKES

Be bop a lu la!

*Why couldn't
the athlete listen to her music?*
Because she'd broken a record.

Where can you play elastic guitar?
In a rubber band.

What instrument goes 'ring ring'?
A saxo-phone.

What kind of music do balloons hate?
Pop.

How do you make a bandstand?
Take their chairs away.

How do you clean a flute?
With a tuba toothpaste.

What is Beethoven doing in his grave?
De-composing.

What food is essential to good music?
Beets.

Why did the music teacher need a ladder?
To reach the high notes.

Where did the music teacher leave her keys?
In the piano.

What do you call a musical automobile?
A car-toon.

How do you get cool music?
Put your CDs in the fridge.

What is a rabbit's favourite dance style?
Hip hop.

Why was the musician arrested?
Because he got in treble.

What makes music on your head?
A head band.

What is the loudest pet?
The trum-pet.

What is a computer's favourite music?
Disc-o.

What is Tarzan's favourite Christmas song?
Jungle-Bells.

THE QUEEN'S QUEENLY JOKES

Now that I've met the queen (and you haven't - ha ha) I thought I'd put in a few jokes for her. Then she can buy a copy of this book for a million pounds. In fact, if she bought 5 copies, that'd be £5 million for me.
Whoopee!

Why did the queen draw straight lines?
Because she was the ruler.

Why did the queen go to the dentist?
To get her teeth crowned.

How do you find King Arthur in the dark?
With a knight light.

Knock Knock
Who's there?
Neil.
Neil who?
Neil down before the queen.

What kind of wood is a queen?
A ruler.

We are not amused.
Take this boy to
the tower and
chop off his head.

IAN'S INKY JOKES

Ian wants to be a writer when he grows up, so this is to make sure he makes me the hero of his books.

What did the pen say to the pencil?
What's your point?

What do you get when you cross a library and an elf?
A shhh—elf.

What has a spine but no bones?
A book.

What's the difference between a boring teacher and a boring book?
You can shut the book up.

What do young ghosts write their homework in?
Exorcise books.

Who makes the best bookkeepers?
People who borrow your books and don't return them.

How do you start writing a book about ducks?
With an intro-duck-tion.

What did one pencil say to the other?
You're looking sharp.

TED'S TIDY JOKES

Oh no, no way, get away from me, Ted, your stupid smelly baby jokes will appear in my book over my dead body. No chance, toad, so get out of— What's that? You'll pay £2 for every joke I include? Well, well, Ted, my friend, step right up, it will be a pleasure to include your jokes.

What did the mummy broom say to the baby broom?
It's time to go to sweep.

Ted, gimme £3 or that joke is out.

Where does a broom go when it's tired?
It goes to sweep.

Make that £5 – your jokes are awful.

Why do witches fly on broomsticks?
Because Hoovers are
too heavy.

Why was the broom late?
He over-swept.

**That does it. £7 cold hard cash –
or else.**

What can't be untied?
A rainbow.

How does a vampire clean his house?
With a victim cleaner.

Have you heard the joke about the dustbin?
Well don't listen, it's a load of rubbish.

The things I do for money . . .

PETER'S PERFECT JOKES

Mum! Henry's trying to make me pay him for putting my jokes in the joke book.

Henry! Don't be horrid.

Peter has pouffy pants, Peter has pouffy pants.

Muuuuuuuuum!

Henry, this is your final warning. Be nice to Peter or no TV for a week.

Humph. It's so unfair.

Psst, everybody, just skip these rotten jokes. Just 'cause I put them in doesn't mean you have to read them. Sometimes you have to make sacrifices for cold, hard, cash.

Who stole the soap?
The robber ducky.

See what I mean?

Why did the belt go to jail?
Because it held up some trousers.

Of all the brothers in the world, I had to get him . . .

What do you get when you cross a camera with a mouse?
Cheese.

How do hedgehogs play leapfrog?
Very carefully.

What happens if you eat yeast and shoe polish?
Every morning you'll rise and shine.

What did the snail say when he was riding on the tortoise's back?
Wheeeeee!

Groan.

Where did Noah keep his
bees on the Ark?
In the arc-hives.

Remember, everyone, Peter's jokes have nothing to do with me.

What was the snail doing on the motorway?
A couple of miles a week.

Peter! That's so dumb!

Isn't!

Is. Pay me an extra £2.

No! Muuuuuuuuum!
Henry's being mean to me.

30

Shut up, Peter.

You shut up, Henry.

Muuuuuuuum!

Peter told me to shut up.

Muuuuuuuuum!

Henry told me to shut up.

Did not!

Did too!

What kind of flower grows on your face?
Tulips.

Stop! **Stop!** That's enough terrible jokes.
Stop! Emergency! Help!!! Bad joke alert! Danger! Danger!

Phew. He's finished. Panic over.

AL'S AEROBIC JOKES

Al says I owe him loads of cash which is completely not true because he ate more of the sweets than I did, but - okay, I'll let him put in a few sporty jokes for free.

What's the hardest part about sky-diving?
The ground.

Why do you have to take two pairs of socks to golf?
In case you get a hole in one.

How can you make an apple puff?
Chase it round the garden.

What's a golfer's favourite letter?
Tee.

Why should bowling alleys be quiet?
So you can hear a pin drop.

How long does it take
for a gymnast to get
to class?
A split
second.

Which sport is always in trouble?
Bad-minton.

What does the winner of a race lose?
Her breath.

What's a horse's favourite sport?
Stable tennis.

What animal is best at hitting a baseball?
A bat.

Why does a wrestler bring a key to the match?
To get out of a headlock.

Why do basketball players love biscuits?
Because they can dunk them.

What drink do wrestlers like?
Fruit punch.

Why is it so hot in a football stadium after a match?
Because all the fans have left.

When is cricket a crime?
When there's a hit and run.

Why can't you tell a joke while ice-skating?
The ice might crack up.

FLUFFY'S FLUFFY JOKES

Mum said I had to let the family contribute to the book. And Fluffy's family, right? I'd rather have Fluffy's jokes than Peter's, any day.

What's yellow and hops up and down?
A canary with hiccups.

What does a cat go to sleep on?
A catterpillow.

What's big and hairy and flies at 1200 miles per hour?
King Kongcorde.

HENRY: Where do fleas go in winter?
FLUFFY: Search me.

What kind of cats love water?
Octopusses.

What are cats' favourite animals?
Mice.

Why did the farmer call his horse Blacksmith?
The horse kept making a bolt for the door.

What's Fluffy's favourite colour?
Puurrrple.

Two cows are in a field. One says 'moo' and the other says 'I was just going to say that.'

What do you get if you cross an elephant with a kangaroo?
Holes all over Australia.

Why do fish live in salt water?
Because pepper makes them sneeze.

How do you make a goldfish age?
Take out the 'g'.

Why did the cat get arrested?
Because of the kitty litter.

How does a dog say how?
He howls!

What do you call a dog on a beach?
A hot dog.

*What do you call
an elephant that flies?*
A jumbo jet.

Two cats were crossing the English
Channel: One, Two, Three and Un, Deux,
Trois. Which one won?
One, Two, Three,
because Un, Deux,
Trois, Quatre Cinq!

NICK'S NEW OPERA JOKES

After keeping me up all night with that horrible opera karaoke, I think Nick owes me big time. So come on Nick, pay up.

Ok Henry, I'll give you £1 if you put in a joke for me.

£1? To put a joke in my fabulous joke book? No way.

All right, seven jokes. And I'll buy a copy to give to my sister for her birthday.

Nick, it will be a pleasure to include your jokes. (I'm rich!!!!!)

How many sopranos does it take to change a lightbulb?

Three. One to do it, one to understudy her, and one to say she could have done it better.

How many tenors does it take to change a lightbulb?

Three. One to do it, and two to say it's too high for him.

How do you save a tenor from drowning?

Take your foot off his head.

Why did the opera singer have such a high voice?
She had falsetto teeth.

What's the difference between a soprano and a piranha?
Lipstick.

What's a snake's favourite opera?
Wriggleto.

MRS ODDBOD'S ODD JOKES

Tee hee. I think I'll collect the cash from Mrs Oddbod *before* I let her read these teacher jokes. Tell them to *your* teacher at your own risk!!!!

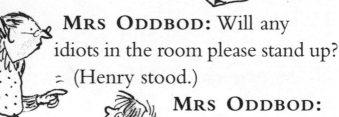

MRS ODDBOD: Will any idiots in the room please stand up? (Henry stood.)

MRS ODDBOD: Henry, why do you think you're an idiot?

HENRY: Actually I don't, but I hate to see you standing there all by yourself.

Why did Miss Lovely have to wear sunglasses?
Because her pupils were so bright.

What happened when Miss Battle-Axe tied the class's shoelaces together?
They went on a class trip.

What happened to the plant in Henry's maths class?
It grew square roots.

How do bees get to school?
On the school buzz.

Why was the clock sent to Mrs Oddbod's office? Because he was tocking too much.

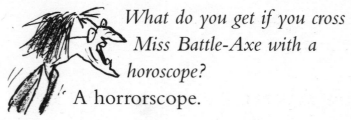

What do you get if you cross Miss Battle-Axe with a horoscope? A horrorscope.

MUM: Does Miss Battle-Axe like you?

HENRY: Like me? She loves me! Look at all those Xs on my test paper.

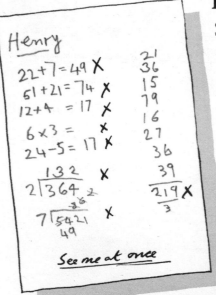

Henry

$22 + 7 = 49$ ✗   21/36

$51 + 21 = 74$ ✗   15

$12 + 4 = 17$ ✗   79

$6 \times 3 =$ ✗   16

$24 - 5 = 17$ ✗   27

$2\overline{)364}$ → 132 ✗   36

$7\overline{)5421}$ ✗   39

$\overline{219}$ ✗ / 3

See me at once

46

RUDE RALPH (on the phone): My son has a bad cold and won't be able to come to school today.

SCHOOL SECRETARY: Who's this?

RALPH: This is my dad speaking.

MISS BATTLE-AXE: Henry, what are you going to be when you leave school?

HENRY: An old man.

MISS BATTLE-AXE: Henry, you aren't paying attention to me. Are you having trouble hearing?

HENRY: No, I'm having trouble listening.

MUM'S MUMMY JOKES

I've put Mum down for 150 books, so that's her Christmas shopping solved.

Why was the mummy so tense?
She was all wound up.

What kind of girl does a mummy take on a date?
Anyone he can dig up.

Why did the mummy leave her tomb after 1,000 years?
Because she thought she was old enough to leave home.

What are a mummy's two favourite kinds of music?
Ragtime and wrap.

How can you tell if a mummy has a cold?
He starts coffin.

Why couldn't the mummy come outside?
Because he was all wrapped up.

How do mummies hide?
They wear masking tape.

Why don't mummies take vacations?
They're afraid they'll relax
and unwind.

What did Tutankhamun say
when he got scared?

I want my mummy.

DR DETTOL'S DOCTOR JOKES

Dr Dettol owes me some cash after that mean trick she played on me with that injection . . .

What did the doctor give the patient with a splitting headache?
Glue.

Why was the doctor always angry?
Because he had no patients.

Why did the window see the doctor?
He was having window panes.

A woman poisoned herself last week eating a daffodil bulb. The doctors told her she would be all right and will be out in the spring.

What does the dentist call her x-rays?
Tooth-pics.

How many psychiatrists does it take to change a lightbulb?
Just one, but the lightbulb has to really want to change.

Why did the banana go to the doctor?
Because it wasn't peeling very well.

Why are fish so easy to weigh?
Because they have their own scales.

Who do fish go to see when they're not feeling well?
The Doctopus.

SiD'S SOGGY JOKES

Hmmn, Soggy Sid, world's worst swimming teacher. Still, I'm sure he'll want to contribute to this great cause, 'Save a child'– I just won't mention that *I'm* the child . . .

In which direction does a chicken swim?
Cluck–wise.

What is a polar bear's favourite stroke?
Blubber-fly.

Why did Miss Battle-Axe jump into the pool? She wanted to test the water.

Why wasn't Sour Susan scared when she went swimming and saw a shark? Because it was a *man*-eating shark.

Why can elephants swim whenever they want? They always have their *trunks* with them.

DR JEKYLL'S
SPOOKY
JOKES

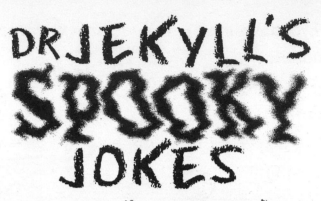

Scaredy-cats **beware!** Don't read these jokes when you are all alone, it's dark out, and there's a strange, scratching noise coming from inside the—

What do you do with a green monster?
Wait until it ripens.

What did one tomb say to another tomb?
Is that you, coffin?

What's the scariest position on a football team?
Ghoulie.

What subject did the witch get an A+ in?
Spell-ing.

Why was there thunder and lightning in the lab?

The scientists were brainstorming.

Where does Dracula stay in New York?
The Vampire State Building.

How many ears did Captain Kirk have?
Three: a left ear, a right ear and a final frontier.

Which vampire tried to eat James Bond?
Ghouldfinger.

What's the first thing that vampires learn at school?
The alphabat.

Why did the vampire enjoy ballroom dancing?
Because he loved the vaultz.

What's a vampire's favourite food?
Scream of mushroom.

What is Dracula's favourite fruit?
Neck-tarines.

What's a vampire's favourite animal?
A giraffe.

Why was the vampire thin?
He ate necks to nothing.

What do zombies eat with bread and cheese?
Pickled organs.

GRETA'S GREASY JOKES

Demon dinner-ladies beware! These yucky food jokes will send everyone screaming from lunch.

What's the best thing to put in a pie?
Your teeth.

What did one crisp say to the other?
Want to go for a dip?

What's green and round and goes camping?
A boy sprout.

What did the sushi say to the bee?
Wasabee.

What do ghosts spread on bagels?
Scream cheese.

In which country do people's tummies rumble the most?
Hun-gary.

Who writes nursery rhymes and squeezes oranges?
Mother Juice.

Where did the burger take his date?
The meat ball.

What's the strongest vegetable in the world?
Muscle sprout.

What do you call a nervous celery stalk?
An edgy veggie.

Why didn't the hotdog star in the film about funfairs?
Because the roles weren't good enough.

What is the best day to have a barbeque?
A Fry-day.

What kind of cake do you get after school dinner?
A stomach-cake.

What happens when you sit on a grape?
It gives a little wine.

OUCH!

Why did the bacon laugh?
Because the egg
cracked a yolk.

*What do you call a dog
on fire?*
Hot dog.

*What did the biscuit say
when it got run over?*
Oh, crumbs.

*Where do fruits play
football?*
A football peach.

What did the mayonnaise say to the fridge?
Shut the door, I'm dressing.

Why did the orange cross the road?
Because he wanted to become orange squash.

Why does Greasy Greta eat bits of metal all day?
It's her staple diet.

On second thought, maybe I won't tell Greasy Greta about this book, after the trick I played on her . . .

SKELETON SKUNK JOKES FROM TJ FIZZ

Hurray! I wrote to my favourite author, TJ Fizz, and she sent me these wicked skeleton and witch jokes.

Why didn't the skeleton eat the food at restaurant le Posh?
Because he didn't have the stomach for it.

What does a skeleton order at a restaurant?
Spare ribs.

What did the skeleton say when his brother told a lie?
You can't fool me, I can see right through you.

Who was the most famous skeleton detective?
Sherlock Bones.

What instrument do skeletons play?
Trombone.

Why do witches wear name tags?
So they know which witch is which.

When do witches cook their victims?
On Fry Day.

Who was the most famous witch detective?
Warlock Holmes.

What do you call two witches who share a room?
Broom mates.

What do you call a skeleton who won't get up in the mornings?
Lazy bones.

Why did the witch consult an astrologer?
She wanted to know her horrorscope.

Why did the skeleton cross the road?
To get to the body shop.

Why did the skeleton laugh?
Because it had a funny bone.

Why couldn't the skeleton cross the road?
He didn't have the guts.

STEVE'S STUCK-UP JOKES

I know Steve will
love these jokes,
because he is so
stuck-up and
lumpy - ha ha
ha.

What's round and mean?
Steve! Oh all right . . .
A vicious circle.

Why did Steve put a 5 pound note in the freezer?
Because he wanted
cold hard cash.

What do you call
a camel with
three lumps?
Lumpy.

What do you get when you cross a camel
with a kangaroo?
A humparoo.

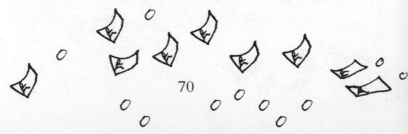

What is green and sits in the corner?
The Incredible sulk.

Yup, that
about sums
Steve up.

Henry, I'm telling
my mum on you.

Go ahead.
Aunt Ruby can pay me to include
the jokes about you, or she can
pay me to get rid of them. Either
way, I'm rich, rich, rich!!!

BILL'S BOSSY JOKES

Next to Steve, Peter, and Margaret, Bossy Bill is one of my worst evil enemies. So here are some bossy jokes just for him . . .

Who is the boss of the hankies?
The Hankie-chief.

Why do dragons make bad bosses?
Because they fire everybody.

CLARE'S CLEVER JOKES

You can't have a
joke book without
some of Clare's
killer riddles. Solve
them and be top of the class.

*If 2 is company and 3's a crowd, what are
4 and 5?*
9.

What has holes, but never spills water?
A sponge.

*What has a head and a tail,
but no body?*
A coin.

What part of the house has a heartbeat and breathes?
The living room.

What goes up but never comes down?
Your age.

What stays in the corner, but travels around the world?
A stamp.

What has a bottom at the top?
Legs.

Why was the computer so good at golf?
Because it had a hard drive.

If an athlete gets athlete's foot, what does an astronaut get?
Missle toe.

What's an eight letter word that only has one letter in it?
Envelope.

What is H2O4?
Drinking.

What has teeth, but cannot eat?
A comb.

What has a head and a foot, but no arms?
A bed.

How many months have 28 days?
All of them.

VERA'S VOMITING JOKES

Tee hee. Vera is the biggest brat I know, but for some reason her parents think she's wonderful. Well, let them put their money where their mouth is. C'mon Polly, pay up or Vera's jokes end up in the bin (where, let's face it, she belongs).

VERA: What's a sick joke?
HENRY: Something you shouldn't bring up in conversation.

What's the best place to have the school sick room?
Next to the cafeteria.

What's the name of the James Bond film where he's sick?
Chunderball.

HENRY'S HORRID JOKES

Yippee! The rudest, more horrid and most disgusting jokes in the book. I've saved the best for last. Prissy worm toad babies beware. These jokes are definitely NOT for you.

Why don't cannibals eat weathermen?
Because they give them wind.

Why do gorillas have big nostrils?
Because they have big fingers.

Why did the lion eat the tightrope walker?
He wanted a well-balanced meal.

*What do you get if you
pull your knickers up
to your armpits?*
A chest of
drawers.

*What did the
submarine say to the ship?*
I can see your bottom.

How does a nit get from place to place?
By itch-hiking.

What do you call a psychic dwarf who has just escaped from prison?
A small Medium at large.

HENRY: There's an awful smell coming from downstairs near Great Aunt Ruby.
DAD: Cellar?
HENRY: Do you think we'd get a good price?

What might you win if you lose ten stone?
The Nobelly Prize.

How do you make a stinkbomb?

Use Peter's underpants.

Muuuuuuuuum!

That's not funny, Henry. Stop being mean to your brother.

Tee hee.

What smells and shoots at people?
A septic tank.

WAITER: I have fried liver, steamed tongue and frogs' legs.
HENRY: Don't tell me your troubles, just get me the menu.

How do you stop a skunk smelling?
Hold his nose.

Knock knock.
Who's there?
Butter.
Butter who?
Butter hurry up – I need the toilet now.

What do you call an exploding monkey?
A baboom.

Knock knock.
Who's there?
Lucy.
Lucy who?
Lucy 'lastic in my pants.

What's the rudest vegetable?
Pea.

Why do giraffes' have long necks?
Because they have smelly feet.

What goes cackle cackle splat?
A witch banging into a lamp post.

Did you hear the joke about the cess pit?
No? Well, it takes a while to sink in.

What's the difference between bogies and broccoli?
Kids don't eat broccoli.

Why did Peter wear nappies to Ted's birthday party?
Because he's a party-pooper.

Mum! He's done it again! He called me a party-pooper in the other book and now he's doing it in this one.

Henry! Don't be horrid.

I'm not doing anything! I'm just adding a few final jokes for my new book.

Mum! They're not funny! Henry is—

84

AAAEEEEEE! Waaaaaaaaaa!

Henry! That's enough! Go to your room.

The End

Thanks to all my friends
who sent me such great jokes!

★

Shahid Ahmed

Sofianne B.

Katy Roes Barrett

Samuel Joseph Berner

Kyle Berry

Kartik Bhargara

Jack Booth

Hugo Chambers

Harry Henry Clarke

Rachel Dodds

Michael Edwards

Damian Fenwick

Garret Gavin

Joshua Hall

Dayleth McKenzie-Manning
David Mitchard
Sarah Jane Paddock
Zofia Rayden
Jemima Ruby Richardson
Luke Seymour
Abba Jessica Sheen
Jack Michael Sheen
Sam James Sheen
Max Shepley
Ibrahim Siddique
Leila Haroon Siddiqui
Charlotte Spratt
Kane Steel
Nathan William Taylor
Harrison Teal
Kelis Wasniewski
Jennifer Williams

HORRID HENRY BOOKS

Horrid Henry
Horrid Henry and the Secret Club
Horrid Henry Tricks the Tooth Fairy
Horrid Henry's Nits
Horrid Henry Gets Rich Quick
Horrid Henry's Haunted House
Horrid Henry and the Mummy's Curse
Horrid Henry's Revenge
Horrid Henry and the Bogey Babysitter
Horrid Henry's Stinkbomb
Horrid Henry's Underpants
Horrid Henry Meets the Queen
Horrid Henry and the Mega-Mean Time Machine
Horrid Henry and the Football Fiend
Horrid Henry's Christmas Cracker
Horrid Henry and the Abominable Snowman
Horrid Henry Robs the Bank
Horrid Henry Wakes the Dead
Horrid Henry Rocks

Horrid Henry's Big Bad Book
Horrid Henry's Wicked Ways
Horrid Henry's Evil Enemies
Horrid Henry Rules the World
Horrid Henry's House of Horrors
Horrid Henry's Dreadful Deeds
Horrid Henry Shows Who's Boss

Visit Horrid Henry's website at www.horridhenry.co.uk for
competitions, games, downloads and a monthly newsletter!